Unbroken Wings-Rise From the ASH.. WIN through Life!

Ashwin Kumar

BookLeaf Publishing

India | USA | UK

Presentation by *BookLeaf Publishing*

Web: www.bookleafpub.com

E-mail: info@bookleafpub.com

ISBN: 9789363316065

First edition 2024

DEDICATION

To the Universe,

I dedicate this book with profound gratitude, recognizing your boundless wisdom and the intricate dance of synchronicity that weaves through our lives. In your infinite embrace, I trust that this book will find its way into the hands of those who need it most, at the precise moment when its words resonate deeply with their souls.

This collection of poems is not meant to be consumed in its entirety but rather savored like a fine wine, with each verse offering solace, inspiration, or reflection as needed. Just as the stars align in the night sky, I believe that the right poem will find its way to the right person at the right time, illuminating their path and offering comfort in moments of darkness.

May this book serve as a reminder of the interconnectedness of all things and the profound beauty of the human experience. With

humility and reverence, I offer it as a beacon of
hope and a testament to the transformative
power of words.

With deepest reverence,

Ashwin

ACKNOWLEDGEMENT

Writing a book is not a solitary endeavor; it is a collaborative effort that draws strength from the support and encouragement of others. With deep gratitude, I extend my heartfelt thanks to those who have contributed to the creation of "Unbroken Wings: Rise From the ASH.. WIN through Life!"

Before I get to thanking the Mortal World, let me thank my 3 spirit Animals:

1. The Dragon—who has always taught me to keep my fire alive inside, never use it unless necessary.

2. The Phoenix—She has been my source of inspiration and helps me live my name Ash-Win... helping me reprise myself every time I have fallen or been put down.

3. The Wolf—I pride myself on being the Wolf, and those I love (my inner circle) as my pack. Loving to protect and nurture them, without leading them from the front, rather being by

their side has helped me gain their unwavering love and support at all given points in time.

First and foremost, I express my profound appreciation to my family and the Wolf pack for their unwavering love and support throughout this journey. Your belief in me has been a guiding light during the darkest of times.

I am indebted to my friends and mentors who have provided invaluable guidance and inspiration along the way. Your wisdom and encouragement have fueled my passion and sustained my pursuit towards my passion for poetry.

I extend my sincere gratitude to the readers who have embraced this book with open hearts and open minds. Your willingness to embark on this journey with me fills me with humility and joy.

Most importantly, I would like to credit and thank the BookLeaf team, the coordinator, designers, editors and rest who seamlessly helped a first time writer like me transition towards completion of this work with little to no hassle. Thank you team for helping me manifest my deeply hidden dream into reality.

I would also like to acknowledge the countless writers, poets, and artists whose work has shaped my own creative vision. Your words have been a source of inspiration and a guiding light on this path of self-discovery.

Finally, I offer my deepest thanks to the universe for the gift of experiences I have gone through in this life and the limitless possibilities it presents. May we continue to soar on unbroken wings, rising from the ashes of adversity to claiming victory in the dance of existence.

With boundless gratitude,
Ashwin

PREFACE

In the tapestry of existence, each thread woven is a story waiting to be told. "Unbroken Wings: Rise From the ASH.. WIN through Life!" is a collection of poems that seeks to unravel the intricate narrative of the human experience—from the inception of life to the final breath.

As we tread the corridors of time, we encounter moments of profound joy and piercing sorrow, moments that shape us and define us. In the pages that follow, you will embark on a journey through the depths of human emotion, exploring the raw and unfiltered essence of what it means to be alive.

Through poetry, we transcend the limitations of language, delving into the realms of the soul where words cease to be mere symbols and become vessels of truth. Each poem within this collection is a reflection of a moment, a feeling, a revelation—an echo of the human heart beating in rhythm with the universe.

"Unbroken Wings" is more than just a collection of verses; it is a mirror held up to the human spirit, reflecting its resilience, its beauty, and its boundless capacity for love and hope. It is a testament to the fact that no matter how dark the night may seem, there is always a dawn waiting to break, illuminating the path forward.

As you journey through these pages, may you find solace in the shared experiences of humanity, may you find inspiration in the triumphs of the human spirit, and may you find the courage to spread your own wings and soar.

With heartfelt gratitude,
Ashwin Kumar

1. Night Before My Birth

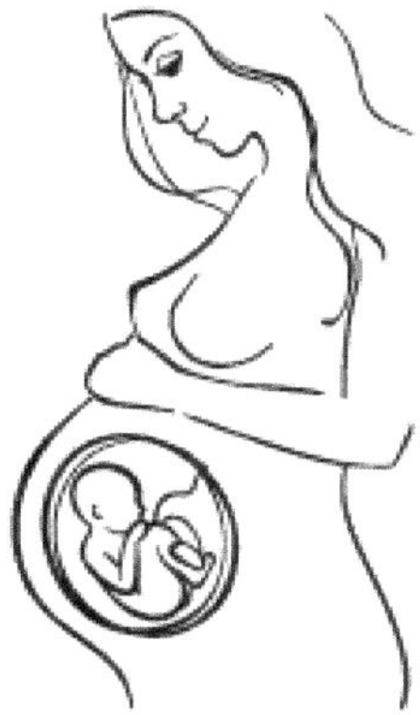

Waited nine months for this night,
Breathless, I cried as my lungs took flight.
Longed to feel, to touch, to see,
Tonight, my Soul is set free!

Yearned to ease my mother's burden,
Prepared to play life's game, never uncertain.
Aspired to soar beyond my father's reach,
Tonight, my Soul is set free!

Enough in this womb, I have moved around,
From this cord, I want to no longer be bound.
Newer ground, across the sea and beyond space
I wish to see
For tonight my Soul is set free!

Restless nights, so close yet far and wide,
Earthbound no more, on this blessed ride.
The eve of my birth, a celestial decree,
Tonight, my soul at last is set free!

About the Poem:

The poem captures the intense anticipation and liberation of a soul on the brink of birth. It reflects a deep yearning to break free from the confines of the womb, expressing the desire to explore the world and embrace life's challenges. The repeated refrain, "Tonight, my Soul is set free!" emphasizes the profound moment of transition from the safety of the womb to the vast, unknown expanse of life. The poem portrays the duality of leaving behind the comfort of the known while eagerly stepping into the limitless possibilities of existence.

2. Who Am I?—A Journey of the Soul

When born, I was called Human
Said I was child of these parents!
Said I was a living being in this world,
So said people, and categorised me as a boy or a girl.
Yet I ask...
Who am I?

Gave me a name,
Taught me this life's game.
But still never said about me,
Still, I myself, didn't know me!
So I ask... Who am I?

Years passed by, I grew old
Made money, bought mansions and gold.
What good with this money I ask
Since I failed in knowing myself, which was a
task!
So I ask... Who am I?

Intellect, brave, lucky they called,
With friends, wife, kids and family, I had it all.
God's blessing on me showered like Niagara
Falls
My question many tried to solve... but alas the
puzzle stood tall!
So I ask... Who am I?

The mother who birthed me, didn't have an
answer
The world that named me, didn't have an answer
The life that famed me, didn't have an answer
The answer to my question, still left
unanswered.
So I ask... Who am I?

God to guide me, I started my quest,
enlightenment's greed, life I now detest.
To seek the answer of who I am.. will be finally
put to rest!
Finally I will now know.... Who am I!!

I got my answer.. finally... it was bold!!
But alas! by me, now it cannot be told.
Gifted my detested life, to the welcoming death
And that is when Death gave me the answer in
my last breath!

I got to know... who I am...
I wish to share the knowledge with thee…
But alas I am no more... as my answer unfolds
my answer to you is untold!
Who am I? Who am I?

About the Poem:

The poem captures a profound journey of
self-discovery and existential reflection. It
explores the universal quest to understand one's
identity and purpose in life, touching upon
themes of societal expectations, material wealth,
and spiritual enlightenment.

The repetition of the question "Who am I?"
throughout the poem creates a sense of
introspection and longing for understanding. It
reflects the inner turmoil of the protagonist as
they grapple with the complexities of their
existence.

The progression of the verses, from birth to death, encapsulates the passage of time and the search for meaning that accompanies each stage of life. The realization that the answer to the question of identity comes only with the acceptance of mortality adds a poignant depth to the narrative.

Overall, this poem is thought-provoking and resonant, inviting readers to contemplate their own journey of self-discovery and the ultimate quest for meaning in life.

3. Fear: A Journey of the Mind

Fear of death, I forgot to live
Fear of loss, I forgot to win
Fear of withering, I forgot to thrive
Fear of forgetting, I forgot them all!

Fear of future, I forgot my past
Fear of past, I forgot my present
Fear of present, I forgot my time
Fear of forgetting, I forgot them all!

Fear of loss, I forgot to gain
Fear of hate, I forgot to love
Fear of ageing, I forgot to grow
Fear of forgetting, I forgot them all!

Fear of shame, I forgot my fame
Fear of tears, I forgot my smile
Fear of doubt, I forgot my trust
Fear of forgetting, I forgot them all!

Let the fear consume, and not let your life
resume,
Let fear fixate fiction, and make you always
assume
Let fear take over your stride, and make your
soul imprisoner for life
For there is nothing to fear but fear itself!
Nothing to fear... but fear itself!

About the Poem:
The poem captures the paralyzing grip of fear
and its insidious effects on one's ability to truly
live and experience life to its fullest. The
repetition of the refrain "Fear of Forgetting, I
Forgot them all!" reinforces the idea of fear
erasing the joys and essential aspects of life.

The structured repetition of different fears
creates a rhythm that amplifies the message,
illustrating how fear permeates every aspect of
existence, from the past to the future, from love
to trust.

The concluding lines offer a powerful reminder
of the self-imposed limitations that fear imposes,
urging readers to break free from its shackles
and embrace life with courage and resilience.

Overall, the poem conveys a universal truth about the destructive nature of fear and the importance of overcoming it to live authentically and fully.

4. Love: A Journey of the Heart

In a fleeting moment, love descends like a dove,
We're enraptured, forgetting all else below or
above.
How does this enchantment seize us, we're often
left in awe,
Only after it strikes do we grasp its wondrous
law.

Parent-child love, a bond pure and true,
Brings a touch of envy even to the divine's view.
From birth to beyond, it stands steadfast and
bold,
A testament to a love from the heavens untold.

Youthful love, like the first summer rain's
embrace,
Will it withstand trials or vanish without a trace?
Infatuation and possession, not love but a guise,
True love sees the soul, beyond what meets the
eyes.

Love for a spouse, a daily sunlit dance,
Bringing joy, not a burden, at every glance.
Binding souls beyond flesh, beyond mortal task,
In this union, love is all we need to bask.

And love for the divine, how do we display?
By loving, living, letting all souls have their say.
For in each of us, the divine does reside,
Let love illuminate, our hearts as our guide.

True love is not just words in a rhyme,
It's a melody that grows sweeter with time.
So let us love, live, and rejoice in this dance,
For true love is found in each loving glance.

About the Poem

"True Love: A Journey Through the Heart", this
poem delves into the multifaceted nature of love,
exploring its manifestations across different
stages of life and relationships. From the pure
and unconditional bond between parent and

child to the passionate embrace of youthful romance, the verses traverse the spectrum of human emotions and experiences.

Through lyrical prose, the poem contemplates the essence of love and its significance in various aspects of existence. It delves into the complexities of love, distinguishing between fleeting infatuation and enduring devotion, and celebrates the transformative power of love that transcends boundaries of time and space.

With each stanza, the poem invites readers on a reflective journey, encouraging them to contemplate their own experiences with love and the profound impact it has on their lives. It serves as a reminder of the beauty and resilience of the human heart, and the universal longing for connection and belonging.

"True Love: A Journey Through the Heart" is not merely a collection of verses; it is a testament to the enduring power of love to inspire, heal, and transform lives. It is an ode to the eternal quest for love and the unbreakable bond that binds us all together in the tapestry of existence.

5. Nightwalker

"Listen to me story," said the Innkeeper,
Called all his crew and customers
joined the jovial drunk and the silent weeper,
A story of the "Nightwalker" that I remember.

With the leather cap and pants of tweeds,
Bright white shirt, and golden buttons
He was the General's Bodyguard Lead,
With his trademark red cape, made of satin.

He was a loyal friend to all, since he was
orphaned since day one,
Being a perfectionist at his work, he stood tall,
as Godfather he had none.
But this lead him to his downfall, straight trees
are cut first you see,
"Strange but true, you will see," said the
innkeeper with a glee.

His friend who was a tramp,
Was in love with the General's daughter.
The General of course heard of this sham,
Ordered for the tramp and his daughter to be
slaughtered.

For his friend, the Nightwalker stood by, as he
knew the pain of having no one
Hid the tramp from them deadly knives, and the
sweltering canons
Put his own life in danger without a sigh, with a
tear in his eye and lips with a smile.
Blinding the soldier's bloodshot eyes.

The tramp and his love had to elope,
To a place, where they'd live fear free and happy,
that was the Nightwalker's ultimate goal and
hope,
With his mighty thought and in God's belief!

He took them both out during a moonless night,
Only galloping horses sound filled the skies,
Wish our Nightwalker's luck was bright,
Alas! It wasn't, for this night is when he was to
die.

Yes! The General discovered this plot,
and called the Nightwalker a traitor.
So, the Nightwalker was stabbed, lynched and
shot,
but all this happened much much later.

For our Nightwalker succeeded,
In giving the couple a happy ending.
Nightwalker didn't mind on how his death was
treated,
For he was there as Best Man for his friend's
wedding.

Even today, during the Moonless night,
in despair and loss of hope, if you need a loyal
friend
You can feel within, the presence of Nightwalker
For his loyalty towards those in need, never
ends.

"Ha! Tis' Horseshit," said the drunk,
I'll bet me last dime, what said is junk.
Hey! Where did the innkeeper go? I got no clue,

Tis' like as though, out the window he flew!"

Hey! Look out the window, screamed someone,
Eyes froze, at the sight they saw, everyone
stunned.
For indeed, he was truly the loyal one.
As even today for you as a friend always he will
be the one!

With his bravery flaunted with his trademark red
cape
And his valour to work symbolised by his
sun-kissed white horse,
not a single galloping sound escaped
And now all knew it was his ghost

Even today he lives by his words
of being there for anyone in need
Don't take me to be absurd when I say
For I have seen him, I know he is here to stay.

About the Poem:

Nightwalker is a narrative poem that unfolds in
the intimate setting of an inn, where the
mysterious innkeeper regales his audience with a
tale of bravery, sacrifice, and the enduring power
of friendship. Through vivid imagery and
emotive storytelling, the poem transports readers

to a world of intrigue and danger, where the enigmatic Nightwalker, adorned in a leather cap and satin cape, emerges as the central protagonist.

"Nightwalker" is a testament to the timeless themes of loyalty, sacrifice, and the resilience of the human spirit. Through its rich imagery and evocative storytelling, the poem leaves a lasting impression on readers, reminding them of the profound impact one individual can have on the lives of others.

6. Never Ending Tracks

In the echo of the train's shrill call,
I embark upon this journey unknown,
Gazing through the window, raindrops fall,
As iron wheels churn, with a melancholy tone,
I traverse these never-ending tracks.

City lights fade into the night's embrace,
Enveloped by the monsoon's chill,
Each raindrop, a reminder of time and space,
A fleeting moment, a silent thrill,
I journey on these endless tracks.

My Love's voice, a distant refrain,
Echoes of a heartache I can't contain,
Body without bone, her words like a chain,
In the depths of loneliness, I find my pain,
I unravel on these ceaseless tracks.

Witnessing disparity, wealth and woe,
Nature's grandeur, mingled with filth,
Inspired yet burdened, wanting to bestow,
But powerless, consumed by guilt,
I navigate these boundless tracks.

Longing for the warmth of loved ones' embrace,
Aching in the solitude of my sojourn,
Assured by whispers from a higher place,
To shield them from harm, my spirit yearns,
I endure along these interminable tracks.

A solitary traveller, transient and alone,
Forming fleeting connections, then they're gone,
In the shadows of those who've flown,
I mourn the bonds that I've outgrown,
I journey on these everlasting tracks.

To those who stood by me, steadfast and true,
I vow to return, stronger when I do,
For now, my life's a voyage anew,
On this train I board, my path to pursue,
I journey forth on these infinite tracks,

In the never-ending embrace of the tracks.

About the Poem:

"Never Ending Tracks" is a reflective and emotive poem that delves into the journey of life, symbolized by a train voyage. Through vivid imagery and introspective narration, the poem explores themes of solitude, longing, resilience, and the passage of time.

The poem begins with the protagonist boarding a train, embarking on a journey into the unknown. As the train moves forward, the narrator observes the changing scenery and experiences a range of emotions, from the melancholy of separation to the longing for connection with loved ones left behind.

Through encounters with disparity and injustice, the protagonist grapples with feelings of powerlessness and guilt, yet finds solace in the assurance of a higher purpose guiding their path. Despite the transient nature of relationships formed along the way, the narrator remains steadfast in their commitment to return to loved ones with renewed strength and purpose.

The repetition of the phrase "never-ending tracks" emphasizes the cyclical nature of life's journey and the inevitability of change and transformation. It serves as a poignant reminder of the constant motion and evolution inherent in the human experience.

Overall, "Never Ending Tracks" is a poignant exploration of the human condition, inviting readers to reflect on their own journey through life's ups and downs.

7. Why?

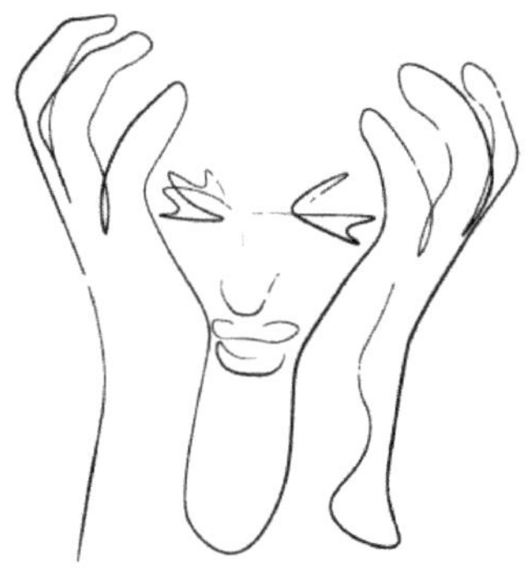

Why does death trail life's fleeting breath?
Why does sorrow linger after joy's flight?
Why does hate shadow Love's tender caress?
Why does every answer beckon yet another
"Why?"

Doubts creep in, where theories thrive,
Anger simmers, beneath sadness's guise,
Suspicion lurks, where trust takes a dive,
And still, the endless "Whys?" perpetually rise.

Hunger gnaws, at the heels of poverty's plight,
Misery clings to the hoarder's grasp tight,
Tears threaten to stain happiness's light,
Each "Why?" a knot in the fabric of night.

Why does inequality sow its bitter seed?
Why does greed devour our noble creed?
Nature's bounty, yet we heedlessly bleed,
Drifting apart, forgetting our mutual need.

Why do we slumber when we should be awake?
Why tread willingly toward our own fate?
Blaming all but ourselves for the path we take,
Blinded to the explosion of our self-made state.

Why does each "Why?" birth another "Why?"
A labyrinth of queries beneath the sky.

About the Poem:

This poem delves into the fundamental questions
that haunt the human mind, exploring the
intricacies of life's paradoxes and the relentless
pursuit of understanding.
Through a series of rhetorical questions
beginning with "Why?", the poem probes the
interconnectedness of opposing forces such as
life and death, joy and sorrow, love and hate.

The repetition of "Why?" creates a sense of
urgency and introspection, inviting readers to
contemplate the mysteries of existence and the

complexities of human emotions and
relationships.
Each stanza presents a new dichotomy, painting
a vivid picture of the dualities that define the
human experience.

The poem delves into themes of existentialism,
introspection, and the quest for meaning,
challenging readers to confront the uncertainties
and contradictions inherent in life.
It encourages deep reflection and philosophical
inquiry, inviting readers to grapple with the
profound questions that shape our understanding
of the world.

8. Seven Deeds

In the vast expanse where stars gleam bright,
I journeyed forth on my soul's twilight flight.
Beneath me, the Earth vanished from sight,
As I soared alongside the Milky Way's light.

In the celestial court, a line stretched far and
wide,
Awaiting my turn with trepidation inside.
An angel's smile, serene and wide,
Offering reassurance in the cosmic tide.

"Am I awake or in death's embrace?"
I asked, bewildered in time and space.
The angel's voice, gentle and grace,
Echoed softly, "You're in a sacred place."

Deeds were weighed, both good and ill,
In the balance of life, a delicate skill.
Equal they stood, an impartial chill,
Yet a chance remained, a flicker still.

"One more chance," the angel's decree,
A reprieve granted, for now I see.
To heaven's gate, a path for me,
But seven deeds must guide my plea.

"SHARE, SMILE, FORGIVE," the first trio,
Kindness bestowed, a radiant show.
In their embrace, love's overflow,
Transforming darkness to a golden glow.

"LIVE, LET LIVE, CARE FOR ALL" the next
decree,
Embrace the world with empathy free.
Each soul uplifted, a symphony,
As unity thrives in harmony.

"Love," the final decree, pure and grand,
A beacon of light in life's shifting sand.
With love as guide, the heart's command,
I traverse the cosmos, hand in hand.

In the realm below, my deeds unfurl,
A testament to love, a sacred swirl.
From Earth's embrace to heaven's pearl,
Seven deeds, a soul's eternal twirl.

About the Poem:

"Seven Deeds" is a poetic exploration of the journey towards self-discovery and redemption, set against the backdrop of a cosmic landscape. Through vivid imagery and introspective narration, the poem takes readers on a spiritual odyssey, guided by the protagonist's encounter with celestial beings and the assignment of seven transformative deeds.

As the poem unfolds, the protagonist's transformation is depicted through their interactions with others and their deepening understanding of the interconnectedness of all beings. Each deed becomes a stepping stone towards personal growth and transcendence, leading the protagonist towards a profound realization of the transformative power of love.

Ultimately, "Seven Deeds" serves as a poetic allegory for the human experience, exploring themes of morality, redemption, and the universal quest for meaning and enlightenment. It inspires readers to reflect on their own actions and choices, and to embrace the transformative potential of love in their lives.

9. True Love

In awe, he feels her radiant grace,
Though blinded by love my eyes can't see your
face.
"I submit to your essence," he whispers,
His hands reaching out, though his sight falters.

Your voice, a melody in my silent world,
I listen with my heart, where emotions swirled.
"In your touch, my spirit finds its song,"
Our love, profound and deep, where we both
belong.

"Shame on you," came my scornful voice,
For judging with eyes that lacked true rejoice.
"Look within, feel the inner lore,"
Startled, they turned, wondering why I was so
sore.

To my surprise, what met my gaze,
Was a love beyond what eyes could chase.
For she was deaf and he was blind,
And me a critical fool not comprehending it in
my mind.

Their union, a testament to love's true form,
Where sight and sound matter not in the norm.
In their embrace, Heaven's light did shine,
A love transcendent, divine and fine.

The critic in me, taken aback by the sight,
Realized love's truth in their shared plight.
For in their world of darkness and silence,
True love blossomed, a radiant defiance.

Sing of true love, O friends, with me,
For in their hearts, it finds its decree.
As my poem draws to a gentle end,
Let true love on our spirits ascend.

About the Poem:

"True Love" is a poem that explores the depth
and resilience of love beyond physical barriers.

It follows the journey of a blind man and a deaf
woman who, despite their individual challenges,
find solace and connection in each other's
presence.
The poem begins with the blind man expressing
his admiration for the woman's beauty, not
through sight but through the senses of his heart
and soul.
As their love unfolds, they are met with the
skepticism of a critic who fails to see beyond
superficial appearances.
However, upon realizing the true nature of their
love and the obstacles they've overcome, the
critic is humbled and acknowledges the beauty
of their bond.
The poem concludes with a message of
celebration for the enduring power of true love,
which transcends physical limitations and shines
brightly in the face of adversity.

10. Echoes of Gratitude: The Poet's Secret Tribute

Poetry, a vessel of our innermost thoughts,
In simple verse, our joys and sorrows wrought.
In times of high or low, it's our release,
In its embrace, all other worries cease.

We ink our beliefs, our praises to the divine,
We mourn the fallen, their stories entwine.
Life, death, eternity—all find their place,
In the tender lines, of the poetic grace.

Let's express our love in poetic refrain,
Describe the grace of the dove and its gentle
reign.
Let's channel messages from realms above,
Through poetry, we share our deepest love.

We cherish crafting poems, but do we pause,
To write an ode for poetry's cause?
What words can capture its essence, its gleam?
How can we honor poetry's silent stream?

"Thank you," I whisper to poetry's embrace,
For translating dreams, in every case.
For poets, it's a dance of thoughts untold,
For me, it's the sun, its warmth, its hold.

So, thank you, poetry, for being our guide,
In moments of joy, in moments we hide.
From literati to fools, you resonate,
In every soul, your beauty, innate.

This dedication, oh poetry, to you I send,
To you, the muse, the beginning, the end.
With gratitude, this poem I dedicate,
For filling my soul with your wondrous state

About the poem:

This poem serves as a metaphor, depicting the
act of self-appreciation and gratitude through the
lens of poetry.
In this allegorical exploration, poetry symbolizes
the self, capable of shouldering the burdens and

responsibilities of others yet often neglecting its own needs and contributions.

Through the imagery of poetry as a vessel for expressing emotions and experiences, the poem underscores the importance of recognizing and honoring oneself amidst the demands of daily life.
It highlights the tendency to overlook one's own worth and the necessity of taking a moment to acknowledge the strength, resilience, and compassion inherent within.

The allegory invites readers to reflect on their own capacity for self-sacrifice and empathy, urging them to carve out space for self-care and appreciation amidst the ceaseless giving to others.
It serves as a gentle reminder that while extending kindness and support to others is commendable, it is equally vital to extend the same kindness and gratitude inward, towards oneself.

Ultimately, this poem is a plea for self-acknowledgment and self-love, wrapped in the metaphorical embrace of poetry, inviting readers to pause, reflect, and offer gratitude to the self for all it does and all it is.

11. Chiseled Tales: Unraveling the Sculpture's Story

In darkness dwells he, solitary and forlorn,
No soul in sight, not even his own shadow worn.
Drowning in tears, in anguish and in sorrow,
Convinced he is, that he won't see another
morrow.

Lost friends to pride, their absence starkly clear,
No one left to lend a hand, no comforting ear.
Time slips away, as if mocking his plight,
The certainty grows that he won't see the light.

Love lost to ego, regrets echo loud,
Moments and memories, like a heavy shroud.

Her voice lingers in his heart's hollow,
Yet he believes, he won't see a tomorrow.

An earthly vessel, never touched by day's
embrace,
Now bound for realms beyond time and space.
Reflecting back, he sees a statue of stone,
How long he endured, remains unknown.

Was this his beginning? Is this the end?
What was his purpose? Did his soul transcend?
Is this the beginning of the end's relentless
trend?
The answers lie with you, my dear friend.

About the Poem

The poem delves into the depths of solitude,
regret, and existential questioning, painting a
vivid portrait of a character facing the
culmination of their journey.
It navigates between the literal and
metaphorical, leaving room for interpretation
and introspection.

The central figure, whether interpreted as a
stone-hearted individual or a literal stone
sculpture, serves as a poignant symbol of human
experience.

Through their struggles with loneliness, pride, lost love, and existential uncertainty, they invite readers to reflect on the complexities of life and the inevitability of mortality.

The poem's enigmatic nature, particularly in line 15 where the protagonist is described as a "sculpture of stone," prompts readers to consider various interpretations and perspectives.
This ambiguity invites readers to engage with its themes on a personal and reflective level.

Thought-provoking exploration of the human condition, offering insight into the complexities of emotion, identity, and existence.
It encourages readers to ponder life's mysteries and confront the ultimate questions of purpose and meaning.

12. Demons

As the dusk sets in, dimming the light,
And birds head to their nests for the night,
As the world twists in their beds left and right,
My demons awaken and gain their might.

A sleepless soul, tormented by thoughts so cold,
Black and white was life, or so I was told,
But it was false; I dare be now bold,
As my life is colored in blood and fiery gold.

Blood of sadness and pain,
Gold were the fleeting moments of gain.
Mind flickering from wrong to right,
I stay wide awake as the world sleeps at night.

My demons awaken,
And my soul is shaken.
My life they have taken,
And sleep for me now, is forsaken.

I close my eyes and shed tears so bright,
Eyes open too, tears flow with all their might.
Try to avoid overthinking, I slip into the
blackness of night,
Wishing I could give up this fight.

Awake at all times, never asleep,
Haunting memories and words give me the
creeps.
Awake or not, I cannot stop this weep,
For my pain is unknown, like an iceberg's deep.

I talk a lot during the day, so people say!
Laughter-filled talks are my mainstay.
Making people happy, in their glee and sway,
In happiness, I wish for them to stay.

Until dusk sets in! Oh Lord, why? I pray!
My tired eyes await dawn's break,
Then this nightmare will end, I hope to stake.
Someday, Angel of Death will take me, I say,
And let me sleep at the eternal stake.

Dying within while alive are my demons,
Winning this game are my demons.

Wondering when it will end, and when did it begin?
For now, my soul is just ASH… WINning are my demons!

About the Poem
"Demons" serves as a metaphor for the experience of depression, portraying it as a relentless, insidious force that awakens with the onset of night. The poem likens the internal struggle to a sleepless, tormented soul battling an array of dark, conflicting thoughts, symbolized by the stark contrast between "blood" (pain) and "fiery gold" (fleeting joy). The speaker's inability to escape these inner demons, despite outward appearances of normalcy and cheer, mirrors the deceptive calm often maintained in public while suffering privately. The poem poignantly encapsulates the profound sense of hopelessness and resignation that accompanies depression, emphasizing the difficulty of finding peace amidst the pervasive darkness.

13. Rise of the Phoenix

Am unhappy with me,
In the mirror I dislike what I see.
In life a loser I feel to be,
In life nothing is all I feel.

Why do you say so? Little one.
Life for you has just begun.
You talk as though you hit a dead end,
your song of life, is yet to be sung.

Dislike my appearance,
dislike the fact that my lover
is writing a poem about me, over
this fact, I feel trapped in my mind's terror tower.

No my Love, do not feel that way,
I just tried to guide you and say
Sun isn't flawless, it has spots but also has rays
Life isn't beautiful without flaws and mistakes.

To know the value of knowing something
beautiful,
you have to know its flaws and mistakes.
To have your life seen as bountiful and fruitful,
the bad with the good you need to take.

To me you are blissful, you are my all,
my uprise and also my downfall.
It is because of you I stand tall.
Love thyself, I say. That is all.

I do not wish to listen to what you feel
for me, I am just unhappy about me.
For I have a mental block now
Just like a lock with no key.

Love thy self, my love, before I die, I say
Don't let your emotions on you run astray.
Negativity is filling you like the hellish plague,
your confidence and trust it will upstage.

Begone! For your words, no more I care,
and the threats of you dying gives me no scares.
"Plague," "Love thy self" Huh! Yes, indeed
Go away, leave! I need no one to preach!

I know what I wish to be,
It is this life, being denied to me,
Frustration and anger in me it evokes,

and now your words have gotten me provoked.

No my love, poison runs in my bloodstream,
had thoughts like you, to myself I was mean.
Consumed it for then, right it seemed,
wasted a life, letting the devil reign in me
supreme!

Alas! My Love, to you my intentions were pure
and clean,
To you, I did not wish to be mean.
Mean I was to me I guide only the right to thee...
Not to provoke you… not even in my dreams.

Love thy self, which I stand by,
Closing on me, are my overburdened eyes.
Love thy self, and rejoice
My heart to you I give, as my time to leave has
come by!

"No, my love, do not do this.
my world will now be engulfed in abyss.
Oh my Lord! Let this not be our final kiss
I love myself, awake now at least!

Alas! How I failed to understand you,
now that I did, you aren't here for me.
To see how I love myself for loving you
True to myself, our love and you! I do!

I shan't die or cry, my Love
will carry your words to people in need.
From the seas below, to the skies above,
Love thy self, to all will spread in deed.

Sniff! Love thy self shall spread indeed.

About the Poem:

"Rise of the Phoenix" is a poignant exploration
of self-love and the internal struggles many face
in accepting themselves.

The poem unfolds as a dialogue between two
voices, one expressing deep-seated insecurities
and the other offering guidance and support.

The protagonist begins by expressing
dissatisfaction with themselves, feeling trapped
in a cycle of self-criticism and negativity.
They struggle to see their own worth and are
resistant to the idea of self-love, even as their
partner tries to encourage them.

The partner, represented as a voice of reason and
compassion, gently reminds the protagonist of
their inherent value and potential.

They emphasize the importance of embracing both the flaws and strengths that make up a person's identity, and urge the protagonist to love themselves unconditionally.

As the dialogue progresses, tensions rise as the protagonist pushes back against the partner's words, feeling overwhelmed by their own internal struggles.
However, the partner persists in their message of self-love, even as they face the prospect of separation.

In the end, the poem takes a poignant turn as the partner departs, leaving behind a legacy of love and wisdom to be shared with others.
Despite their absence, their words continue to resonate, inspiring the protagonist to embrace self-love and spread the message to others in need.

Overall, "Rise of the Phoenix" is a reminder of the importance of self-acceptance and compassion, and the transformative power of love in overcoming internal struggles.
It serves as both a call to action and a testament to the enduring impact of genuine care and support.

14. Whispers of the Heart: Unveiling the Unknown

In the realm of her thoughts, a girl so lost,
Smiled a façade, yet within her thoughts tossed.
Perceived as bold, the world couldn't behold,
The layers within, countless stories untold.

Then came a guy, a surprise unforeseen,
Who swept her off, as if from a dream.
His mission clear, to unearth her true smile,
To illuminate her soul, if only for a while.

"Why?" she questioned, her skepticism ripe,
Suspicious of motives, doubting the hype.
"What good do you seek for me?" she implored,
"Leave me be," her emotions floored.

He smiled, his touch a gentle balm,
In his arms, she found a sense of calm.
"Let me show you," he began to croon,
In a love song, under the moon.

"My dear love, let me reveal to you,
In the melody of a love so true,
If you're the poem, then I am the verse,
Your essence profound, my words immerse.

"If you're the heart, then I am the beat,
Together, a rhythm, harmonious and sweet.
In chaos, I'll be your tranquil shore,
Against life's tempests, together we'll soar.

"I'm no hero, just a devil at best,
But for you, I'd face any test.
To see you truly live, to witness your joy,
I'd brave any storm, any ploy."

Moved by his words, tears filled her eyes,
Yet they weren't tears of pain, but of joy's ties.
For in him, she found solace, her guide,
Her devil, her angel, forever by her side.

"Doubt no more," he whispered near,
"Let our love story be crystal clear.
You're not alone, for I am your light,
Together, we'll conquer any plight."

And so, in his embrace, she found her peace,
Her doubts dispelled, her fears released.
For in his love, she found her home,

Their love story, forever to roam.

About the Poem
This enigmatic poem delves into the intricacies
of love, identity, and self-discovery.
It follows the journey of a girl who, though
seemingly confident and strong, hides a world of
complexities beneath her facade.
When a mysterious guy enters her life with the
intent of unraveling her true self, she is initially
resistant, questioning his motives and the
possibility of a genuine connection.

However, as he persists in his efforts to show her
kindness and affection, she begins to soften,
gradually allowing him to break down her walls
and reveal her vulnerabilities.
Through a symbolic love song, he expresses his
deep and unwavering love for her, likening their
relationship to the intricate components of music
and poetry.

As the girl's skepticism turns to acceptance and
joy, she realizes the depth of the guy's love and
his role as her confidant and partner.
Together, they embark on a journey of mutual
understanding and acceptance, embracing their
love story with gratitude and optimism for the
future.

Overall, the poem explores themes of trust, vulnerability, and the transformative power of love to heal and bring joy.
Through its lyrical language and evocative imagery, it invites readers to reflect on the mysteries of the human heart and the profound connections that shape our lives.

15. Monsoon Memories: Love's Downpour

As the monsoon descends upon the earth,
Grey skies cloak the land in a misty rebirth.
The gentle breeze whispers of love's refrain,
And amidst the rain, you find me smiling again.

"Why do you smile so?" she asks, curious and
mild,
Each raindrop, to me, feels like a love compiled.
I meet her gaze, my heart skipping a beat,
For her, my smile is an ode, sweet and complete.

My love, you are my first monsoon rain,
Quenching the thirst of my soul's barren terrain.
Like a desert yielding to an oasis' touch,
Your hand in mine, healing hurts that were such.

Your eyes, akin to clouds, pristine and bright,
Your smile, a lightning bolt, igniting the night.
Through the heat and the storm, you're my
sanctuary,
With your tender raindrops, you set my smile
free.

Your drops, a balm to my eternal thirst,
Not of love alone, but of care, genuine and
immersed.
Each touch, a caress that penetrates deep,
In your rain, my hidden tears find a keep.

In your embrace, my tears find a silent ally,
As you pour down, my sorrows begin to dry.
Cease only when my smile gleams anew,
Then, like sunlight, shine on, even when skies
are blue.

Oh, my first monsoon rain, how you assuage my
pain,
No longer do I endure life's scorching disdain.
Your arrival, a promise kept in due time,
Now, within me, you flow, a sweet, soothing
rhyme.

Through the trials of time's relentless trial,
You arrive, a gentle breeze, to make me smile.
Each raindrop, a pearl in a necklace, so rare,

A gift I shall string, for you, my love, to wear!

You are my rain, my sunshine, and much more,
Your love, a downpour that my heart adores.
I sing this ode, my heart's humble score,
To you, my love, for my heart is sore no more.

About the Poem

This poem captures the transformative power of
love through the metaphor of the monsoon rain.
It begins by painting a vivid picture of the
arrival of the monsoon, with its grey skies and
gentle breeze setting the scene for the emotions
that follow.
The speaker compares their beloved to the first
monsoon rain, symbolizing the renewal and
healing that their presence brings.

Throughout the poem, there is a sense of
gratitude and awe for the love shared with the
beloved, portrayed as a source of comfort and
renewal in times of sorrow and pain.
The imagery of tears being hidden by the rain
adds a layer of vulnerability and intimacy to the
portrayal of the relationship, highlighting the
depth of the emotional connection between the
speaker and their beloved.

As the poem progresses, the speaker expresses
their love and appreciation for the beloved,
likening them to a precious gift and promising to
cherish and honor their love.
The imagery of raindrops forming pearls and the
promise to string them together as a gift adds a
romantic and poetic touch to the expression of
affection.

Overall, the poem captures the beauty and depth
of love, portraying it as a force of nature that has
the power to heal, renew, and bring joy even in
the darkest of times.
Through its rich imagery and heartfelt sentiment,
the poem resonates with the reader, inviting
them to reflect on the transformative power of
love in their own lives.

16. Dance of the Dragon & Phoenix

In the crowded hall, we were a world apart,
Two souls entwined, beating as one heart.
Amidst the noise, our silent symphony,
She, my phoenix, I, her dragon, in harmony.

Her eyes met mine in an unspoken vow,
In their depths, the dance of the phoenix's flame
I avow.
As we moved to the rhythm, a celestial trance,
Our spirits soared, caught in fate's dance.

Through the night, I prayed for time to stall,
Hoping our union would endure, standing tall.
But destiny's hand, a cruel decree,
Tore us apart, breaking our unity.

In a fleeting moment, our love was lost,
A rift appeared, our bond the cost.
I held back my confession, let silence reign,
Now we're apart, destined to feel love's pain.

With the break of dawn, she'll walk away,
To another's arms, her heart will sway.
Yet in this moment, our souls still entwine,
In the dance of the dragon and phoenix, divine.

Though she'll belong to another's embrace,
Tonight, in this dance, we find solace and grace.
Let the music weave our souls' romance,
In the eternal dance of the dragon and phoenix's
trance.

About the poem:
"Dance of the Dragon & Phoenix" delves into
the profound complexities of love, destiny, and
the intricacies of human connection.
The title evokes imagery of two mythical
creatures engaged in a mesmerizing and
symbolic dance, reflecting the intertwined
destinies of the poem's protagonists.

Throughout the verses, the poem navigates the
emotional landscape of a fleeting yet deeply
meaningful encounter between two individuals.

Their union is likened to the powerful and mystical dance of the dragon and phoenix, each representing strength, passion, and transformation.

Despite the fleeting nature of their connection and the challenges they face, the protagonists find solace and grace in the moment they share. Their dance becomes a symbol of resilience, as they navigate the twists and turns of fate's design.

The poem captures the universal themes of longing, regret, and acceptance, inviting readers to contemplate the complexities of love and the inevitability of destiny.
Through vivid imagery and emotive language, it paints a vivid picture of the human experience, resonating with anyone who has ever experienced the profound highs and lows of romantic entanglement.

Overall, "Dance of the Dragon & Phoenix" is a poignant exploration of love's transcendent power and the enduring nature of the human spirit, wrapped in the mystical embrace of myth and symbolism.

17. From Flame to Darkness: A Farewell

And there she goes,
With her flowing chi glow,
Away from me she grows—
Being one with her was my curse and
blessing, joy and sorrow.

She flows away with a smile,
Which I missed to share for a while.
Only for her did I stay alive,
For our promised tomorrow, today I
sacrificed.

I deserve pain;
My tears drench my soul like the monsoon
rain.
Yet, I have something bigger to gain—
The sight of you leaving, showing no
restraint.

Punishing me, the heavens above,
I deserve it for not being around.
But none can love you the way I did, my
love;
This I declare from my grave and beyond.

The fire in me was not worth your life,
Hurt I am, yet I wish you happiness while
my smile survives.
I wish I had been the one to make you sing
and rhyme,
Nonetheless, I thank you for sharing your
life in my borrowed time.

My death now nears—
Death, once feared, now dear.
I have no one, I have none.
Come, my dear Death, embrace me; I am
done.

For no one else is here to hold me now,
As she was the last to embrace my life
somehow.
No one can see my inverted frown,
Masked beneath a lively smile.

These are the words of the dying wick,
Watching the candle bleed as its last bit of
wax drips.

Without her, I am just burning with no hope;
Death embraces, darkness engulfs, as their
love story ends.

About the Poem

"From Flame to Darkness: A Farewell" is a
poem that captures the emotional intensity
of loss and resignation. It uses the
metaphor of a dying candle to symbolize the
speaker's fading life and the end of a
profound love. The poem vividly portrays
the speaker's inner turmoil, blending themes
of sacrifice, regret, and acceptance with
evocative imagery. The repeated references
to fire and wax enhance the metaphor,
illustrating the transition from vibrant life to
inevitable darkness. The speaker's reflective
tone and acceptance of death, coupled with
a final, heartfelt farewell, convey a powerful
message of enduring love and the somber
reality of parting. Overall, the poem
effectively marries emotional depth with a
consistent and resonant metaphor. Isn't this
also what our Souls might be telling to our
melting body? Perhaps, is this the reason
why the Soul remains and the body
perishes?

18. Return to my realm

In your presence, I was blind to the depths of my love,
Now, without you, memories refuse to fade,
soaring above.
Death holds no fear, dreams lose their gleam,
Oh, my love, return to me, fulfill my desperate dream!
Return to my realm.

You are the essence of my soul, my reason to survive,
Yet your love for me has ceased to thrive.
Empty are my arms without your embrace,
Why must I endure this torment? Come back to my space!
Return to my realm.

Should death claim me, I fear losing you
forevermore,
Yet in life, I bleed from the wound you tore.
Why must I suffer this agony, my Lord, this
pain?
What solace can I find? Come back, break this
chain!
Return to my realm.

Though my eyes remain dry, my heart weeps
silently,
Withering away in your absence, you see not, so
empty.
I'll close my eyes, and in dreams, you'll be near,
If not in this life, then in the next, my dear.
Return to my realm.

As you rest on my lap, peaceful and serene,
Yet oblivious to the turmoil within, unseen.
How can I endure without you by my side?
From death's grip, from dreams, return, let love
abide!
Return to my realm.

About the Poem
The Poem delves into the profound depths of
yearning and despair experienced by the speaker
in the absence of their beloved.

The poem navigates through a spectrum of
emotions, from the initial disbelief and denial to
the eventual acceptance of the painful reality.

The repetition of the plea "Return to my realm"
serves as a poignant refrain, echoing the
speaker's desperate longing for the return of their
beloved.
Each stanza delves deeper into the speaker's
emotional turmoil, exploring themes of love,
loss, and existential questioning.

Through vivid imagery and heartfelt
expressions, the poem captures the essence of
heartache and longing, inviting readers to
empathize with the speaker's plight.

It conveys the universal experience of yearning
for connection and the pain of separation,
resonating with anyone who has felt the ache of
a lost love, and in the end, it is realized that the
love was not lost due to a fight, but the lover
was no more and this is the irreversible plight.

19. Eternal Twilight: A Love Beyond Time

In the twilight's embrace, where sun and
mountain meet,
She ascends the castle's edge, her heart's fervent
beat.
For eons, this moment she did pine,
As I unfurl my love's wings with a smile divine.

My touch, a wintry frost, yet warmth it yields,
Her spine shivers, yet her blush bravely shields.
Oudh's fragrance surrounds, I'm mesmerized,
entranced,
As she leans close, my heart's rhythm she's
dance.

She favors wine, crimson like the human's vein,
While I cherish the hue of love's eternal reign.
She offers her neck, a silent plea in her eyes,

I kiss her gently, with lips alone, no fangs or
disguise.

Centuries apart, her youth a fleeting bloom,
But in her love, my ancient soul finds room.
Her pure affection breaks immortality's curse,
In her embrace, I find solace, my universe.

As dawn approaches, we bid our sad adieu,
Her hand in mine, watching skies turn blue.
With each sunrise, I fade to dust's embrace,
Her tearful kiss, my final resting place.

But fear not, beloved, for I shall return,
In spring's bloom, a dandelion's yearn.
In winter's chill, I'll be your steadfast fern,
Our love, a flame that will forever burn.

At dusk, she waits, her heart's silent call,
For a vampire's love, the greatest of all.
Together we'll soar beyond mortal wonder,
A phoenix and dragon, in love's eternal thunder.

About the Poem:

The poem is a narrative that explores the
timeless and transcendent nature of love, set
against the backdrop of a mystical and
enchanting world.

It tells the story of two lovers, one immortal and the other mortal, whose love defies the boundaries of time and mortality.

The imagery employed throughout the poem is vivid and evocative, drawing the reader into the fantastical setting of sunsets, mountain castles, and eternal love.
The use of sensory details, such as the fragrance of Oudh and the taste of wine, adds richness and depth to the narrative, engaging the reader's senses and immersing them in the experience.

The poem captures the emotional intensity of the lovers' bond, from the longing and passion they share to the bittersweetness of their inevitable parting.
Despite the challenges they face and the passage of time, their love remains unwavering and enduring, symbolized by the promise of reunion and eternal devotion.

Overall, the poem is an exploration of love's power to transcend time and mortality, weaving together elements of romance, fantasy, and longing to create a truly enchanting and poignant tale.

20. Echoes of Emptiness: Navigating the Soul's Abyss

In the chaos of my wounds, I once thrived,
As pain bled from me, I felt alive.
Amidst the dance of demons, I stood alone,
In crowds, yet solitary to the bone.

But now, as healing slowly finds its way,
I'm adrift in a void, lost in disarray.
Peace, once sought, now feels like a tomb,
And I dread the silence of this lonely room.

Caught between darkness and light's embrace,
I tremble, suffocating in this endless space.
Each breath a burden, heavy with despair,
As I navigate this existence, stripped bare.

I taste the bitterness of numbness, no sensation,
See the world through eyes clouded by
frustration.
Living a life devoid of vitality's trace,
A wasteland of emptiness, a barren place.

With all I had, I fled, I ran,
Now adrift in time, with no past or plan.
I glimpse the flicker of life's fleeting span,
Feeling like nothing more than a castoff can.

The nights refuse to grant me peaceful sleep,
Daylight dawns with promises it cannot keep.
This life clings to me, unwilling to let go,
While death eludes, denying me its final blow.

In this paradoxical existence I reside,
Yearning for release, yet still I bide.
I turn to you, oh God, in hopes of grace,
To grant my weary soul a resting place.

We all wage battles, face demons within,
Life's not a race, nor a quest to win.
Find your pace, embrace the journey's grace,

In its twists and turns, find your sacred space.

Separated we thrive, in sanity's embrace,
Together, insanity's grip we cannot face.
But within the spaces, in chapters we nurse,
We find solace in wounds that disperse.

This mortal coil, a tapestry of joy and woe,
Teaching us the irony that only death may know.
Yet in facing life's myriad faces, we find grace,
And through God's plan, we navigate this maze.

As I write these words, fear and faith collide,
In the depths of my imagination, I seek to hide.
Yet amidst the chaos, I summon courage anew,
To face another day, and bid the world adieu.

About the Poem

The poem delves into the profound complexities
of the human psyche, portraying a poignant
journey of healing amidst inner turmoil.
It navigates through themes of loneliness,
existential angst, and the relentless pursuit of
solace, painting a vivid picture of the struggles
and triumphs inherent in the process of
overcoming mental and emotional challenges.

The ninth stanza stands out with its clever wordplay, where the term "insane" is dissected into "in sane." This linguistic device serves to underscore the delicate balance between sanity and madness, highlighting the notion that within the chaos of one's mind, there exists a semblance of clarity and rationality.
By emphasizing the "in" within "insane," the poem suggests that even amidst the madness, there is a space for healing and restoration.

Furthermore, the poem poignantly captures the idea that the journey towards healing is often fraught with pain and discomfort.
The speaker grapples with the agonizing process of confronting their inner demons and navigating through the darkness of their own thoughts.
Yet, despite the overwhelming challenges, there is a steadfast determination to persevere, fueled by the belief that the end result will be worth the struggle.

Ultimately, the poem serves as a powerful testament to the resilience of the human spirit and the transformative power of self-discovery and acceptance. It underscores the importance of acknowledging and embracing one's vulnerabilities, and the courage required to

embark on the journey towards healing. Through
its evocative imagery and introspective
narrative, the poem resonates with readers,
reminding them that while the path to healing
may be arduous, the rewards of inner peace and
self-fulfilment are invaluable.

21. Silent Scream

It's easy to react in fleeting moments,
Leaving scars that time cannot erase.
Why endure the torment others inflict,
Allowing dark demons to claim their space?

Hell isn't a realm beyond life's end,
It hides within, a shadowy friend.
The space between my ears, a private hell,
Where pain waits, and demons dance so well.

Words may seem innocent, their intent unclear,
Yet to the suffering, they echo as fear.
Perception can turn a spark into a blaze,
Burning bright within the shadows' haze.

A bruised soul feels every word's weight,
Unseen wounds can seal a cruel fate.
Sanity seeks normalcy, but madness grows,
In unseen realms where the dark thorn shows.

Parents, teachers, friends, and love,
All can break, none may mend.
A spell cast, unyielding, confronts,
Karma tallies the soul's end.

We reap what we sow, intentional or not,
Earthly hell's wrath from birth to lot.
So heed each action, from dawn till dusk,
For what we sow, reaps hell's fiery trust.

Death may seem the easiest to face,
But it would end with too much grace.
Keep me alive, torment both day and night,
The demons' power, their cruel delight.

When demons grasp and hollow the soul,
The once bright light dims, losing control.
Left alive for their relentless play,
The same light burns until the last day.

Few know the depths of truest pain,
Only those who've felt it truly remain.
No one can traverse this maze alone,

Without mercy or grace to guide us home.

Cut flesh, broken bones, numbness' trace,
Yet the mind's torment knows no surface space.
Those who end their silent cry are not weak,
Just souls too shattered to speak.

If someone drifts, a stranger in the fray,
Don't add to their torment or push them away.
Pray for their healing, stand by their side,
A prayer, a smile, might turn the tide.

Not just to live, but to rise and thrive,
To love again, to see hope alive.
To smile anew beyond tears and sighs,
Finding reasons to live, despite the cries.

Reason to live, a quiet scream,
For those trapped in this nightly dream.
Demons seek to end our soul's light,
We hold on for loved ones, one more night.

About the Poem

"Silent Scream" delves into the profound inner
turmoil experienced by individuals who grapple
with emotional pain and mental suffering. It
portrays the internal "hell" that manifests

through tormenting thoughts and the impact of
seemingly innocuous words and actions, which
can amplify the anguish of those already
struggling. The poem emphasizes the cyclical
nature of suffering and karma, urging empathy
and support for those in distress. It
acknowledges the harsh reality of mental
suffering compared to physical pain, while also
expressing a resilient hope to find reasons to live
and rise above the darkness, despite the
relentless grip of inner demons.

22.Rainathon

The wetness of drops,
As my worries take flight,
In the rain's gentle crops.

The sound of rain
Drowns all my pain,
Its soothing murmur
Wraps my soul in a chain.

Oh, Rainathon, I say,
Your name's a mislead,
It's more than a shower,
It's a prayer, indeed.

My walk aligns with thought's pace,
Breath quickens, heart's race,

The rain, a thief of my stress,
As my busy life finds its solace.

Tears blend with these tender drops,
Sweat hides the bruised mind's stops.
In the rain's embrace, I always find gain,
My wait for its grace has never been in vain.

If life feels like it's let you down,
See how clouds break to wash sorrows around.
Part from yourself, let your blood pour as rain,
To bring calm to your soul, and soothe your
pain.

So if you're not someone's sun, moon, or star,
Nor the sky, or a distant planet afar,
If you feel lost in the crowd's might,
Look back—perhaps you're someone's cloud,
pouring hope of life.

About the Poem

"Rainathon" explores the deep comfort and
emotional renewal found in rain, portraying it as
more than just a natural phenomenon but as a
profound source of solace and healing. The
poem depicts rain as a therapeutic force that

washes away worries and stress, creating a
calming sanctuary where the speaker's pain is
eased. It reflects on the rain's soothing sound
and its ability to align with the speaker's
thoughts, blending personal suffering with
nature's relief. By personifying rain and clouds,
the poem conveys a message of self-worth and
significance, suggesting that even if one feels
insignificant, they may still play a crucial role in
bringing hope and comfort to others.

23. The Night Before My Death

Celebrated my birthday,
Unknown to me,
That this would be my last day,
Oblivious I was... for tonight my soul is set free.

Felt strangely filled but empty,
With people cheering around me
everything felt achieved and complete
Felt it all... for tonight my soul is set free.

Couldn't sleep that night, though eyes shut real tight,
Recalling my life 's journey, flooded with memories
Ups and downs, the love, joys and fights
Awakened I was... for my soul is set free.

Couldn't hear my breath, nor feel the heartbeat within my chest,
Alighted the stairs, I was heading to see the Almighty.
Finally arrived, the night before my death...
Peace I got as I... set my soul free!!

At last... I see my mortal body inert and still, as my soul soars and is set free!

About the poem:

The poem captures the bittersweet moment of celebrating one's birthday, unaware that it will be their last day on Earth. The juxtaposition of joyous celebration with the underlying theme of impending departure creates a poignant atmosphere.

The repetition of the refrain "For, tonight my Soul is set free" throughout the poem serves as a powerful reminder of the inevitability of death and the ultimate liberation of the soul from the confines of the mortal world.

The imagery of feeling both filled and empty, achieved yet incomplete, evokes a sense of introspection and contemplation about the meaning of life and the fleeting nature of human existence.

The final stanza, with its vivid depiction of the narrator's journey towards the afterlife and the release of their soul from their mortal body, brings a sense of closure and acceptance to the narrative.

Overall, the poem captures the emotional depth and spiritual resonance of the journey from life to death, leaving readers with a sense of reverence for the transient beauty of existence.

24. Unbroken wings..
Reprise from ASH to WIN
in Life.

Though fallen to the ground,
I refuse to remain bound.
Like the moon's ascent each fortnight,
I too shall rise and bring day to this night.
I will survive... won't I?

Pushed down countless times,
Yet I rise, a phoenix in my prime.
Like waves against relentless tides,
I'll ride life's roller coaster with pride.
I will survive... can I?

Sloth and greed may sow their seed,
Anxiety and despair may make me bleed.
My wings may break, my spirit may sigh,
But I'll rise again, to touch the sky.
I will survive... will I?

What seems shattered will mend in time,
My wings will heal, and once more I'll shine.
Mark my words, heed my rhyme,
I'll transcend, become divine.
I will survive... should I?

See, I bleed no more,
My wounds are no longer sore.
My heart sings, my spirit sings,
Oh look, my wings are unbroken!

I will survive... with my unbroken wings,
Ready to soar once more.
I'll take flight again,
From ashes I reprise to Win again!
I will survive...!

About the Poem

"Unbroken Wings: Reprise from Ashes to Win" is a powerful poem about resilience and personal transformation. It uses the imagery of a phoenix and unbroken wings to symbolize the speaker's journey through adversity and their determination to rise above challenges. Despite facing setbacks and internal struggles like sloth, greed, and despair, the poem emphasizes the speaker's unwavering resolve to overcome these obstacles and reclaim their strength. Through a cycle of questioning and affirming their ability to endure, the poem ultimately celebrates the triumph of renewal and the readiness to soar to new heights, emerging victorious from the trials faced.

25. To my Soul... With Love!

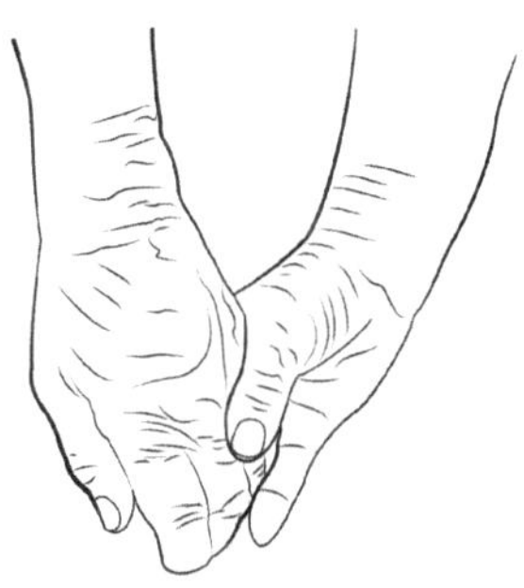

I know I am not perfect,
As you may see through your eyes,
I am not as strong,
As you might feel in your heart's ties.
I am not the best,
As your mind may visualize,
I am not a god,
Yet in me, your spirit lies.

You fell for my imperfections,
And turned them into strength,
You chose me over the rest,
Embracing a devil masked with intent.
You bled for me, as in you I dwelled,
I saved you? Are you insane?

You rescued me from my own dark pain,
You are my eternal flame,
Bringing warmth and light from realms above.

I am not the best, yet you stayed,
For which I thank you from now to forevermore.
I cannot promise life will always be kind,
But I vow never to let you go, not even for mine.

Thank you for saving me from myself, my love,
I have risen from the depths below.
Loving and respecting you is my ultimate goal,
For you are me, and me you, my dear soul.

About the Poem

"Love Letter to Soul" serves as a reminder to
embrace self-love and acceptance. The poet
writes a heartfelt letter to their own soul,
acknowledging personal imperfections and
vulnerabilities while expressing profound
gratitude for the transformative power of
self-acceptance. Through the metaphor of a
partner's unwavering love and support, the poem
emphasizes the importance of recognizing one's
own worth and staying true to oneself. It
conveys that despite flaws and struggles,
self-love is a crucial source of strength and light,

encouraging readers to cherish and respect themselves as an integral part of their journey toward personal growth and fulfillment.

weareunhinggd@gmail.com

*"This journey of one's lifetime is just the
start while the book seems to end...
The Multiverse of lifetimes is yet to unfold...
so stay sharp as very soon we will meet
again and transcend"*